IMAGES
of Scotland

AROUND
HELENSBURGH

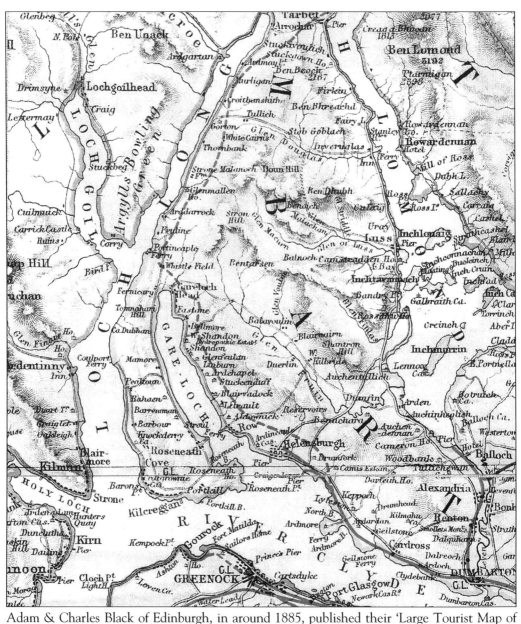

Adam & Charles Black of Edinburgh, in around 1885, published their 'Large Tourist Map of Scotland'. Dissected and mounted on cloth, each of the twelve sections sold for one shilling! This part of the Glasgow, Trossachs and Oban Sheet illustrates all of the places mentioned in this book. The West Highland Railway, shown by a broken line, was under construction from Craigendoran, behind Upper Helensburgh to Garelochhead, Arrochar and Tarbet, and onward. The ferry no longer crosses 'Row Narrows', but the superb situation of Helensburgh can be seen, facing south and with extensive views.

Cover photograph: A fine and lengthy musical tradition in the town is exemplified by this production of Hiawatha's Wedding Feast and Death of Minnehaha on 18 April 1906 at the Victoria Hall. T.W. Stanton is the conductor, seated centre behind the instrumentalists with his wife, Edith, on his right. G.H. Stanton is the cellist at front left and the soloists were Major (later Provost) John F. Duncan and Mrs Hyllested. William Battrum Lever, sometime Provost and keeper of the Sinclair Street Music Shop, played the harmonium.

IMAGES

of Scotland

AROUND
HELENSBURGH

Kenneth N. Crawford and Alison Roberts
for Helensburgh Heritage Trust

Captions by
Kenneth N. Crawford

TEMPUS

First published 1999
Reprinted 2002

Copyright © Kenneth N. Crawford, Alison Roberts
and Helensburgh Heritage Trust, 1999

Tempus Publishing Limited
The Mill, Brimscombe Port,
Stroud, Gloucestershire, GL5 2QG
www.tempus-publishing.com

ISBN 0 7524 1532 8

Typesetting and origination by
Tempus Publishing Limited
Printed in Great Britain by
Midway Colour Print, Wiltshire

The Rhu Church Woman's Guild in the 1930s. The Revd P.W. Lilley with, presumably, the ladies ready to manage the stalls at a sale of work. From left to right: Miss Jessie McKenzie, Mrs McKenzie, Mrs J. Arnold Fleming, Miss Niven, Mrs McDougall and Mrs Lilley.

Contents

When the first Ordnance Survey was made in 1860, Helensburgh was quite well developed but compact. Clyde Street was built from Sutherland Street to Craigendoran Avenue(especially the large houses at that end), and the northern limit of the town was reached at Milligs Street. There was no West Highland Railway, but the Glasgow line had reached East Princes Street.

Acknowledgements

This book has been compiled mainly from albums, photographs and memories, which are the treasured family possessions of members of the Helensburgh Heritage Trust and their friends and from which we have made our personal selection.

The Heritage Trust and compilers gratefully acknowledge the valuable information and additional photographs willingly supplied by: the Helensburgh Librarian and Argyll and Bute Council; *Helensburgh Advertiser* and the Clyde and Forth Press Group; J. Grant, Scottish Maritime Museum; Royal Northern and Clyde Yacht Club; J. Allaway, *Navy News*; G. McFeely, Office of Flag Officer, Scotland and Photographic Section, HMS *Neptune* for Crown Copyright (MoD). The map above is reproduced by permission of the Trustees of the National Library of Scotland. To anyone holding copyright in any photograph which appears and whose consent has inadvertently not been sought, please accept this full apology.

Introduction

By *Norman M. Glen, CBE, TD, JP, MA (1911-2002)*
The last Provost of Helensburgh, 1970-1975

Helensburgh is a town with quite a short history but a wonderfully interesting record expressed in many different fields. In this volume the photographs depict the appearance of the town and its surroundings over the period of its existence – from a Royal Burgh of Barony, which it was created on the twenty-eighth day of May 1802, up to its life as a town living partly by its association with the Royal Navy and partly as a popular home for families with business and industrial interests in Glasgow. Looking forwards, Helensburgh also has a hope for development as a tourist-related centre, due to its location near the future Loch Lomond National Park.

The origin of the town is believed to be the result of a visit to the newly created New Town area of Edinburgh by the Laird of Luss, Sir James Grant or Colquhoun, around 1765. Sir James was so impressed by what he saw there that he resolved to create a planned town on his land on the shores of Malig, opposite Greenock. There was some delay before development started. The name Helensburgh was chosen by Sir James to honour his wife Helen, granddaughter of the Duke of Sutherland. The use of family names is repeated in the naming of many streets in the town, for example, James, John, William, Sutherland and also in frequent use of names that suggest a strong Royalist support as in Queen, Princes, Charlotte, and Adelaide Streets and King's Crescent.

Progress in developing Helensburgh was slow but eventually the town achieved Burgh status. With the election of its first Provost a period of expansion commenced, as did the history of the town as a place with a remarkable record of residents with names known nationally and internationally.

The first name of note to emerge was Henry Bell, best known as owner and creator of the *Comet* steamship, but also a man of vision in seeking to develop the Burgh as a modern town. In more recent times Helensburgh was the hometown of Andrew Bonar Law, long time leader of the Conservative Party and Prime Minister of Great Britain in 1922 until his premature death. The scientific genius John Logie Baird, the inventor of television, was born and educated in Helensburgh and is buried in the town cemetery. There is also a tradition associated with the stage and cinema through Jack Buchanan and Deborah Kerr, and the world of literature is represented at very high level by Sir James Fraser, writer of *The Golden Bough*, and two poets who briefly taught in Larchfield School, W.H. Auden and C. Day Lewis.

This book about Helensburgh displays, in pictorial form, many aspects of a town with a multiplicity of interests. The close links with the sea down through the past 200 years are featured in the sections covering the piers, the passenger ships and the port and submarine base, and it is of special interest to see Princess Diana on board HMS *Trafalgar*. In addition, a section covering army and land based activities during the two world wars is featured.

Local families with a record of public service covering a period of over 100 years are remembered by their continuing influence on the life of the town. They include Andersons (Templetons), the Kidstons, the MacLachlans (who for 109 years were the Town Clerks) and others.

Helensburgh has a proud record of youth at work in organisations such as the Girl Guides, the Scouts and the Boys' Brigade, while the town has always had an interest in sport with a number of Scottish champions on the golf course and tennis courts, not to mention Olympic success in yachting.

Lastly, I have to introduce Helensburgh as a town of great architects and artists. The work of Charles Rennie Mackintosh is beautifully displayed in The Hill House. Many buildings are by Leiper, Thomson and Paterson, and the artistic works of the 'Glasgow Boys' had many links with the town.

A study of this book is in itself interesting and it deserves a follow up in the form of a visit.

From 1802 to 1975 Helensburgh enjoyed Burgh status in its local administration. This 'Welcome' sign of that period is at the entrance least often used by visitors to the town – from Arrochar along the shores of the Gareloch. It is set against Rhu Road Higher and the West Lodge of Dalmore House (1873), designed by William Leiper.

One
Over the Years

The development of West Bay was on the landward side of the main road, and largely of a commercial nature. However, there was no uniformity of height or style so that considerable variety in building may be seen as early as 1880. Row boats are inverted on the shore, and the obelisk to Henry Bell is prominent.

This is the earliest available engraving of the Western Esplanade where the Glennan Burn enters the Firth of Clyde and dates from 1841. The seafront is already well built from William Street to the Pier. The foreground is enlivened by a 'bathing machine' and children with a dog under the care of mother or nursemaid.

Looking towards the pier from the east in 1880 the East Bay curves impressively but, in the town, building had taken place on the seaward side so that both commercial and residential property took the frontage to the Firth away from the road. Nevertheless, a recreation area was infilled and laid out with seats provided, between the private gardens. The tower of St Columba Church is right of centre and St Andrew's is on the left.

From William Street, also in 1880, the view shows the road pot-holed, while the sea wall and grass only start opposite John Street. The garden beyond the first block was of Lady Augusta Clavering's home which was set back. Vittorio's Cafe now occupies the site of the garden.

Rhu Bay is the length of foreshore beyond old Rhu Pier. In the distance 'Ardenvohr' can just be seen, complete with tower and conservatory. It is now the home of the Royal Northern and Clyde Yacht Club. The house had a number of private owners before purchase by the Royal Northern Yacht Club in 1937. The tower was removed, but almost immediately the premises were requisitioned by the RAF for experiments with flying boats in Rhu Bay. Row, Rue and Rhu are different spellings but all pronounced 'Roo' as it is today.

The centre of the town was, in 1880, and still is, one row away from the seafront at Colquhoun Square, an elegant quadrant of lawns and flower beds at the intersection of West Princes and Colquhoun Streets. Looking at the north-western quadrant is West United Free Church, with its door directly into the Kirk. Despite street lighting having been introduced in 1846, only a single gas lamp can be seen to light the whole square.

A 1959 view of Colquhoun Square, looking at the south-eastern quadrant past the Centenary Celtic Cross, towards the Tower Cinema on the extreme right. One of the two town cinemas, this was demolished in 1980 together with Reid's corner shop and the cottages in the centre. They all gave way to a cohesive redevelopment comprising the Royal Bank of Scotland and retail shops, with residential or commercial units – including a professional suite for the architect of the scheme, Alan Berry. When Samuel Bryden was Provost in 1902, the Celtic Cross was sited in the road centre, but with the coming of the motor-vehicle it was considered an obstruction and was moved to the north-west quadrant. Roses, floral beds and seats enhance the square.

St Andrew's (now West Kirk) stands in Colquhoun Square. The original building of 1853 was by Liverpool architect James Hay, to a design with which he had won prizes at the Great Exhibition in 1851. The front porch was designed by William Leiper and added in 1892. A disastrous fire destroyed the roof and interior on 24 February 1924, only the spire and Session House escaping. At the time, there was a vacancy in the Ministry, but the congregation set to and organised a restoration to the same design and ordered a new first-class organ.

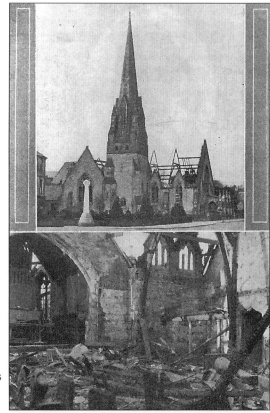

The original half-timbered ceiling and interior shown here was destroyed, but was re-created. The fire damage must have been most disheartening. Subsequently an adaptable performance venue has been provided. The musical tradition of the town is supported greatly by the availability of this well-kept building with its top quality organ and grand piano.

The old parish church was built in 1846 by architect Charles Wilson of Glasgow. In this picture of 1850 an extension is being built - and the Granary is on the left.

The old church and its hall provided shelter to many refugees from the 1940 bombing of Clydebank. Then there was use as a hostel by King George's Fund in connection with the development of the Submarine Base at Faslane, but all uses had ended by 1983 and the decision to demolish was taken. However, the clock tower remains and at its base is the Tourist Information Centre.

The south-western quadrant of Colquhoun Square in 1960, viewed from the tower of St Columba church. From the right of the photograph are the 1893 Post Office with its tall lead-covered cupola, designed by W.W. Robertson, and then the motor repair garage and National Petrol station of Munro & Pender Ltd. The garage and the buildings in Colquhoun Street have been replaced by the second part of the scheme, which now houses professional offices, the *Helensburgh Advertiser* and a cafe. The traditional telephone boxes have since been replaced and relocated near to the Post Office and the site re-used for a community notice board.

Fugie's Yard or 'The Barracks' prior to its demolition in 1885. In 1860 these properties were owned by one of the railway companies to house their navigators or 'navvies' employed on construction works. There were twenty-nine dwellings and late in the nineteenth century its residents were frequently named in court reports. The picture was taken just before demolition in 1895 – could it also show an early protest meeting? This area of James Street was laid out as a children's play area in 1907.

A pier existed from the earliest times and was essential to the early progress of the town as its principal means of access, both from Glasgow and, more importantly, across the water from Greenock. Residents, visitors and goods would all be discharged. This realistic photograph is of coal being landed from a Clyde puffer while the inspector supervises.

Kidston Park, Helensburgh.

Kidston Park was opened in 1877. It seems that the Duke of Argyll had proposed to feu the land for a house to be built, but William Kidston of Ferniegair felt that as this was the last piece of recreational land in the west of the town it should be saved. He obtained a group of supporters and persuaded the Duke to accept a reduced price of £650. Sir James Colquhoun and Mr Kidston each offered to contribute £200, and local residents the balance. Mr Niven prepared a landscaping plan and further contributions were solicited for the laying out. At the time it was known as Cairndow Point. A dispute arose when Sir James wrote that, in his view, the resulting park should not bear the name of any of the contributors. How it now comes to be known as Kidston Park is not clear, although the inscription still on the plinth states that the park was 'chiefly' the gift of William Kidston and that he 'left funds for maintenance.' The structure of the bandstand and drinking fountain have not stood the test of time, but an extensive car park enables young and old to leave the car 'out of town' and walk to the cafes and shops and back along the seafront.

17

West Shandon House in 1903. The house was commissioned in 1852 by Robert Napier to house his collection of books, works of art and rare plants, some of which had been brought here by David Livingstone. Napier was the leading marine engineer of his day and had worked for lighthouse engineer Robert Stevenson. After Napier's death in 1876 the mansion became Shandon Hydropathic Hotel, complete with salt water swimming baths. From 1952 it was used by the Ministry of Defence and only demolished in 1960 to become part of the Clyde Submarine Base.

Only the lodge and part of the boundary wall of the Hydro remain, and for years served as an unusual post office. One of the ponds which supplied the swimming pools is now used by the Model Boat Club.

Ardencaple Castle was built as the family seat of the Macaulay Clan. It passed to Buchanan in 1737 and to Colquhoun in 1862. This aerial view in 1930 shows arable land shortly before development as Ardencaple and Loch Drives parallel, and Cumberland and Castle Avenues at right angles to the seafront. The castle suffered from dry rot and was demolished in the 1950s, save for a square tower and buttressed retaining wall, the former supporting navigation lights for naval and other vessels entering Rhu Narrows. In October 1998 a Gathering was held at which the Honourable Clan MacAulay declared its intention to re-acquire the tower for use as a clan museum.

Hermitage House was the home of the Cramb family who, in 1880, provided part of their front garden for the building of Hermitage Secondary School. Adjacent playing fields became known as Cramb Park. In 1911 the Burgh Council paid £3,750 for the whole property and developed Hermitage Park. The house was used as an Auxiliary Hospital from 1914-1918, and then as a school annexe until the primary school was built. Demolition came in 1963, just after this picture was taken.

Interiors of Victorian houses can be of interest – these are at 'Inistore' (now 'Glenkin'), 72 John Street, where Mrs Annie Anderson is seated at the dining table, which is set for tea, behind a bowl of flowers!

The drawing room in 1891, and Mrs Annie Anderson reads, or recites, to her husband William (sometime Provost) and her sister, Frances Mary Templeton. Frances was an accomplished embroiderer of the Leek School and examples of her work are in the Victoria & Albert Museum collection.

The Hill House, internationally famous as the work of architect Charles Rennie Mackintosh, was built in 1902-1903. It was commissioned by publisher Walter Blackie, who obviously found the interior so liveable-in that no changes were made, and he and his family lived here for fifty years. Mr & Mrs T. Campbell Lawson stayed for a further twenty years and it was in this period that the picture was taken – with children exploring the roof top! The Royal Incorporation of Architects in Scotland recognised the importance of the house in 1972 and managed it for ten years. The National Trust for Scotland now owns the house and contents, which are open daily from April to October, and receive visitors from all over the world. Recently, with assistance from the European Regional Development Fund and Dumbartonshire Enterprise, more rooms have been restored. They are now open to display new domestic design with facilities for interpretation of the work of C.R. and his artist wife, Margaret Macdonald Mackintosh.

St Bride's church in West King Street contained this memorial window to its first Minister, Revd John Baird, BD (1842-1932). Father of John Logie Baird, he had been the incumbent for forty-two years. It was arranged that it be saved and stored following the building demolition and has now been restored by the Heritage Trust and is on display in the Library.

Opposite: Shown here, prior to demolition in 1995, St Bride's Church was built in 1887 (architect: A.N. Paterson). The congregation merged in 1959 with the Old and St Andrews in Colquhoun Square, and then in 1981 a fresh start was made under the current title of West Kirk. The replacement building comprises Housing Association flats surmounted by a new public clock tower and also the new Helensburgh Public Library.

Alma Place was a terrace of artisans' dwellings in East King Street. The redevelopment of four-storey tenements that began in 1937 has recently been modernised and refurbished. Opposite the present police station, and at the corner of Grant Street, the latter now gives access to the two-deck car park which serves the supermarket, railway station and medical centre.

Public toilets are rarely appreciated until no longer available! This small block was at the south-eastern corner of East King and Sinclair Streets until 1982, now the site of Co-op supermarket. Down the street the 1902 extension to Municipal Buildings is just visible, and above is the glazed arch of the canopy over the platforms of Central Railway Station.

The Old Granary was a picturesque building on the sea front facing the old parish church. Originally a malt barn, it fell on hard times but became a bus garage, a restaurant and finally a bingo hall. Demolition was imminent when this photograph was taken in 1981. A replacement building was also known as the Old Granary, but was a public house before being renamed 'Clockworxs'!

Also on Sinclair Street, but opposite at No.77 on the south-western corner, was G. Arthur MacInnes, a gents outfitter and drapery shop called Kings Cross Warehouse. This ground floor is now a solicitor's office.

The firm of Burgess was started in 1878 by Alexander Bilsland who lived on the premises at 13 James Street. In 1893 James Bisland was an artist and teacher at Dumbarton School of Art. Seen here soon after they purchased the business in 1907 are Mr J.G. Burgess and his wife Jane. The business continues in West Princes Street.

This group of buildings in West Princes Street is known as Waverley Place and remains as elegant today as it was in 1910. Street level retail uses change with the times. Clyde Grocers are long gone, as are all other service-based grocery businesses in the town.

A group picture of the staff employed by Helensburgh Steam Laundry in the 1920s. Situated at 55 East King Street, it must in its heyday have had an extensive clientele amongst the wealthy families in the grand residences built in the upper part of the town and also among the hotels catering for visitors. The laundry was closed and demolished in 1966.

The Commodore Hotel survived this disastrous fire in 1978, being rebuilt and extended to become the principal residential hotel within the town – the restaurant and bar have spectacular sea views.

Macneur & Bryden Ltd will be mentioned throughout this work, and would probably have published it, if still in business! The shop front is now Victoria Wine but the gold lettering still exists above that shop and the Lloyds TSB Bank. The firm published the *Helensburgh and Gareloch Times*, the Helensburgh Directory, tourist guides, postcards and general printing. They were booksellers, newsagents, estate agents, and sold artists' materials and sports equipment. There was even a trade in second-hand ice skates in season! Samuel Bryden and Mr Macneur bought the printers' premises from William Battrum in 1875 and the last proprietor, Walter S. Bryden, took over in 1959 and retired in 1980. He was a founder member of Helensburgh Heritage Trust.

Two

Good Works

Helensburgh became a Burgh of Barony by Royal Charter in 1802 with a provost, two baillies and four councillors. It was elevated to Police Burgh in 1846, but in 1975 was incorporated within Dumbarton District Council and Strathclyde Regional Council, although it also then had a Community Council. Further reorganisation in 1996 created unitary authorities and, following an intensive campaign by residents, the town is now within the area of Argyll and Bute Council. Three Grants of Arms signify these changes. They are from the left, those of the Burgh, the Community Council and Argyll & Bute Council. The original Burgh Arms combined those of Sir James Colquhoun and his wife, Lady Helen Sutherland – the black St Andrews Cross, the greyhound, and the motto *Si Je Puis* meaning 'If I can,' and battlecry *Cnoc Elachan* representing 'Armory Hill' were from the Colquhouns. Three gold stars on a red shield and a savage were from the Sutherland side. The stag's head is a symbol of a knights' battle armour and the coronet signified a Statutory Community Council, and now also an Area Council. The Argyll motto *Seas ar coir* means 'Maintain our right.'

The most famous son of the town is probably Henry Bell (1766-1830), and the building most associated with him and his wife was the Baths Hotel. It was built in 1808 and after his death, was managed by his widow for another thirty years. After her death, its name was changed to Queen's Hotel. The conversion in 1984–1986 retained but extended the building to create the present Queens Court residential property. This drawing by Edna M.W. Rae was made in 1934. It is a nice coincidence that the first and last provosts of the town both made this building their home. Henry Bell's great achievement was the launch in 1812 of *The Comet* – the first steam-powered passenger-carrying vessel. She was 42ft long and drew 4ft of water. The flywheel and anvil were displayed in Hermitage Park but in 2002 became a feature of East Bay Esplanade.

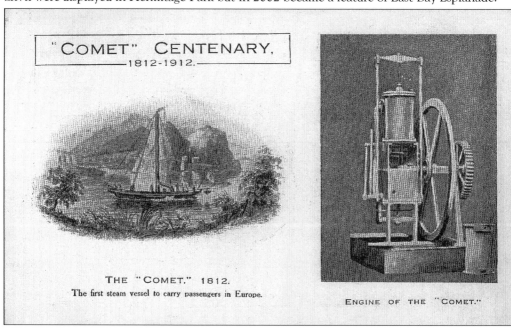

"COMET" CENTENARY,
1812-1912.

THE "COMET." 1812.
The first steam vessel to carry passengers in Europe.

ENGINE OF THE "COMET."

On the centenary of *The Comet* in 1912, Macneur & Bryden published a series of postcards in commemoration. These showed *The Comet*, a model of its steam engine (opposite page), the Obelisk on the sea front (erected in 1872 by the townspeople), the Henry Bell Monument in Rhu Churchyard, The Baths Hotel and, of course, this portrait.

"COMET" CENTENARY.

HENRY BELL,
Pioneer of Steam Navigation and first Provost of Helensburgh.

Macneur & Bryden, Helensburgh.

A little-noticed memorial is the bust of Henry Bell over the door of Municipal Buildings, in that position because he was elected the first Provost of the town, serving from 1807 to 1811.

The commercial retail status of the lower part of Sinclair Street was well established by 1916. On the right is Peacocks' barbers pole, behind it the golden horse indicating Waldies Carriages, while opposite is Spy's coal yard.

A splendid view along East Princes Street from opposite Central Station. From the right of the photograph are the Municipal Buildings (architect; John Honeyman), built in 1878 on the site of the only theatre ever in the town, civic street lamps and the grocery on the corner in a small building. Behind is a three-storey tenement originally intended to turn the corner, but its gable was never quite finished. On the far left is the Post Office at Colquhoun Square.

This portrait is of James Smith of Jordanhill who became the third Provost of the town, 1828-1834. A man of many interests and a patron of yacht designer William Fyfe, he was also an authority on local geology and president of the Andersonian University, which became Anderson College of Medicine in Glasgow. He purchased the Baths Hotel after the death of Henry Bell to allow Mrs Margaret Bell to continue in management.

HELENSBURGH

Municipal Election.

TUESDAY, 6TH SEPT., 1859.

FROM 11 A.M. TILL 3 P.M.

I VOTE FOR

1. ANDREW OSWALD, GLENNAN BANK.

2. JAMES ORR, THORNHILL.

3.

4.

(SIGNATURE.)..

An example of the voting card for the Helensburgh municipal election held on Tuesday 6 September 1859. No secrecy then – the elector had to sign it! Now, 140 years later, elections have been held by 'secret ballot' on 6 May 1999 for members of Argyll & Bute Council and also for members of a new Scottish Parliament.

Reflections in the pool at the War Memorial, which was erected by public subscription in 1923. Designed by local architect A.N. Paterson FRIBA, ARSA, RSW, to a proposal by J. Whitelaw Hamilton, it is sited within a walled garden. Here, in 1967, the civic and services representatives listen to the minister's address. Colour Parties from the services training organisations mount guard.

The War Memorial in Hermitage Park is the scene of the Annual Service of Remembrance each November, which is now organised by the Community Council. In this 1969 picture, Provost J. McLeod Williamson, wearing his Robes of Office, lays a wreath in honour of the Burgh War Dead. Guard Commander Lieutenant John Davies of HM Submarine *Repulse* leads the naval contingent.

Clyde Street School, Helensburgh, was built by Row School Board and was an early design of A.N.Paterson. It was opened by Sir James Colquhoun, Bart, on 9 August 1904. This view was printed by Lindsay Laidlaw Press in the town, and may have been for the invitations to the opening. The wording in the stonework is 'School Board of the Parish of Row Clyde Str. School', and there are separate iron gates and school doors marked 'Girls' and 'Boys.' For some years it has been very successful as a Community Education Centre, with facilities for many voluntary clubs and associations.

The Burgh Council created a putting green on the sea front in 1925, near to the Pier Head. Although remodelled from time to time, it is still in use and is still managed from a timber hut, then near to Colquhoun Street, but now nearer to the Pier. At the time of the opening ceremony the cost of a round was 3d, but is now £1. Tweed 'breeks' and flat caps, as well as starched collars and bow ties, are in evidence.

'Drumgarve', John Street in 1875. Nearly all of the Templeton family appears, but in miniature. They lived in the house from 1870, and the third generation gave it to the Burgh Council in 1946 for use as a public library in memory of William Anderson (1854-1928), and his wife Annie Templeton (1858-1928). The library and reading room continued until 1998, when a purpose-built library opened. The future of 'Drumgarve' is uncertain. Part of these front lawns were developed earlier by the erection of cottages known as Drumgarve Court.

In 1912 all ten of the Templeton family posed for this picture at the door of 'Drumgarve'. From left to right, back row: Rosa, Archie, John and Susie. Middle row: Annie, Frances, Ralph and Agnes. Front row (seated on ground): Lizzie and James with dog Derry. Only Annie married, becoming Mrs William Anderson and bearing five children.

One of the later generation of the Templeton family, Miss Annie T. Anderson MBE, JP, known as 'Nance' (1889-1980). Here she is enjoying a sail on the Gareloch steamer *Lucy Ashton*. Nance was a Town Councillor, Member of the Hospital Board, and County Organiser of the Women's Voluntary Services for Civil Defence. Educated at St Bride's School, Froebel College, Bedford and Oxford University, she became a teacher at St Bride's, founded the first Brownie pack, produced for the Dramatic Society and was President of the Art Club and a Benefactor – all in Helensburgh.

Annie Templeton (mother of Nance) as a young woman (photograph by Fergus of Greenock).

A 1925 drawing of Annie aged sixty-six by Hamish Constable Paterson. He was a noted portraitist and nephew of A.N. Paterson.

Standing are John Preston (b.1864) and Ralph Trimingham (b.1871 in Helensburgh). Seated are Archibald Douglas (b.1865) and James Heriot (b.1862), the four sons of James and Susan Templeton.

Susan Lightbourne Trimingham, wife of James Templeton, an East India merchant. She was born in 1834 in St Johns, Newfoundland, and after marriage lived in Demerara, British Guiana, before arriving in Helensburgh. Most of her ten children were brought up in Helensburgh!

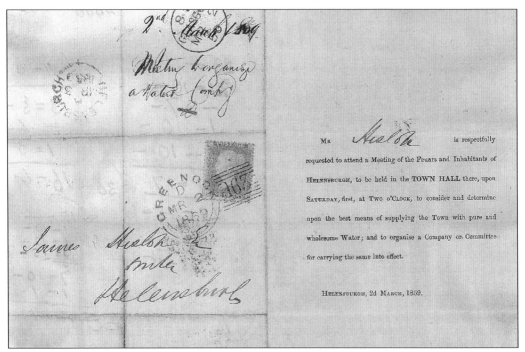

In March 1859, a meeting of feuars and inhabitants was called to decide upon the best way of supplying pure and wholesome water, and thus setting up a Water Company. The first reservoir delivering mains water was opened at Mains Hill in 1868, and four years later enlargement enabled a piped water supply to run to the town from Ballyvoulin.

A feature of life as an elected member of a local authority has always been the Annual Inspection of premises and equipment. It is believed that this group of early motor vehicles is in Sinclair Street preparing to leave the Municipal Buildings for the 1910 Waterworks Inspection.

A tradition of floral planting decorates Hermitage Park. This, in the summer of 1959, commemorated Robert Burns (1759-1796). 'There was a Lad!'

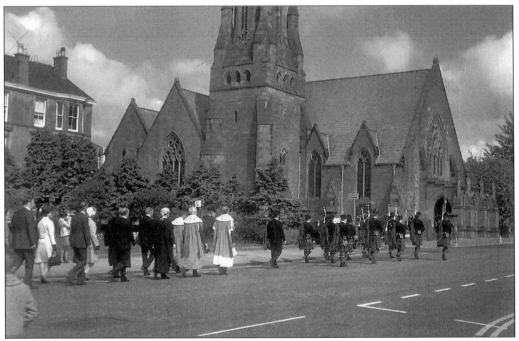

To mark the statutory abolition of Scottish Burgh Councils, Helensburgh Burgh Council, on 11 May 1975, processed from Municipal Buildings to West Kirk. Members and officers of the Council were lead by the Helensburgh and District Pipe Band. An illuminated parchment, signed by the participants on the day is still displayed in the Kirk porch.

The Baird family in 1890. Mrs Jessie Baird (1855-1924) is seated on the right with John Logie Baird, aged two, on her knee. The oldest boy is James (1879-1945), and the two girls are Annie (1883-1971) and, sitting at the front, Jean (1885-1955). This group portrait is by Stuart of Glasgow and Helensburgh, possibly the first professional photographer with a studio in the town.

The Lodge, Argyle Street in 1905. This was then the home of the Reverend John Baird BD, the first Minister of St Bride's church. It is probable that the photographer was their seventeen-year-old son, John Logie Baird, but it is not known who the young man posing for the photograph is.

John Logie Baird had become famous by 1926 as the inventor of a system of transmission of pictures by radio waves – television. Here he is being greeted on the doorstep by his father, the Revd John, and his sister Annie. The dog is 'Jinkie'.

Mrs Annie Templeton (Anderson) tending the garden at 'Inistore' John Street in May 1911.

New Parish Council Chambers.

Lines Written on the Opening of the New Parish Council Chambers, and read by her Husband at the Dinner.

To inaugurate this handsome place
We are gathered here together,
And we are numbered not a few,
Despite the stormy weather.

May peace and harmony ever reign
Supreme at all our meetings.
To every member of the Board
I wish the season's greetings.

I drink the health of all concerned ;
My toast is very brief ;
I hope that all who here apply
Will always get relief.

" More blessed to give than to receive,"
Then let it be our study
To help the sick, deserving poor
With what they need—the money.

Margaret Ross Spy was born in Cromarty in 1845 but married Robert Spy and lived in Glenan Gardens on West Argyle Street. She was a pianist and poet who died prior to 1904. One of her poems is reproduced from the book printed by Macneur and Bryden, and published privately by her husband. This will have been written to mark the completion of the building of the Rhu Parish Council Chambers in West King Street. The administration of the areas outwith the Burgh took place from here. Until recently, Registrars of Births, Marriages and Deaths had offices in the building and the Marriage Room continues in popular use.

Three
Transport and Trippers

A spectacular view of the Firth of Clyde looking across the Clyde towards Helensburgh. An annual day visit on 6 July 1996 by *Queen Elizabeth 2* to the Greenock Ocean Terminal brings out all of the escort vessels. The QE2 is obvious, PS *Waverley* is beyond her bow, nearer the camera is the *Second Snark*, and in the foreground the Caledonian MacBrayne car ferry leaving for Dunoon and using speed to cross ahead of the great liner. Helensburgh Pier is at the extreme right of the background.

A steamer named *Waverley* serving the passenger trade on the Clyde existed in the nineteenth century. This picture is of the third *Waverley*. She was commissioned in 1899, saw service as a minesweeper 1914-18, and was sunk after being dive-bombed at Dunkirk in 1940.

The London & North Eastern Railway had A.& J.Inglis of Glasgow build the fourth *Waverley* in 1947. She was to turn out to be the last paddle steamer built for service on the Clyde, with her maiden cruise on the Three Lochs route via Loch Long and Loch Goil on 16 June 1947. Owned by Caledonian Steam Packet Co. and then Caledonian MacBrayne, she was withdrawn in 1973. However, the Paddle Steamer Preservation Society restored her to service in 1975 and she continues to operate Summer Clyde Coast Cruises but in early and late season also visits English and Welsh resorts. This view shows her leaving Helensburgh Pier, full astern, en route to Glasgow from her Golden Jubilee cruise in Loch Long on 21 June 1997.

Craigendoran Pier in its hey day in the mid 1930s. The North British Railway had provided four steamer berths and a bay platform for the trains from Glasgow. From left to right are *Talisman*, perhaps awaiting a pleasure cruise, *Kenilworth*, *Marmion* and *Lucy Ashton*, whilst *Jeannie Deans* is at sea. The direction indicator shows that boats are sailing for Rothesay, Innellan, Dunoon, Kirn and Kilcreggan. The music business of William Battrum has an advertisement.

A short-lived form of public transport on the River Clyde was a hovercraft, operated by Clyde Hover Ferries from Craigendoran to Largs. This photograph was taken on Largs foreshore in August 1985. Apparently, the waters of the Firth proved to be too rough, and the berthing arrangements adjacent to piers damaged the flexible skirt materials then in use on the craft. Once torn or damaged the ferry lost its ability to hover and shore repairs were required.

Sweeping in to Rhu Pier in 1904 is the PS *Lucy Ashton*, which was for very many years the mainstay of the steamer service between Craigendoran and the Gare Loch. Near to the Pier Master's Office, a carriage awaits an important passenger.

Rhu had the only solid stone-built pier on this part of the Clyde. It opened in 1835 but closed to steamer traffic in 1920. It has not disappeared as it is now incorporated in the Rhu Marina, supporting the yacht lift.

Helensburgh Pier was started in 1816 and lengthened in 1822 but in mid-century was described as one of the worst in Scotland! On 21 March 1844, *The Telegraph* was leaving the pier when her boiler burst with the loss of eighteen lives. Another pier was opened in 1859, extended in 1871 and, in 1897, the pier head buildings were completed. It closed in 1952 but reopened after restoration in 1979 to enable a regular summer service by PS *Waverley*. An all-year-round passenger ferry service connecting with Kilcreggan and Gourock is now operated by MV *Kenilworth*, and it may be that Greenock will be added to the route. The end of pier shelter burned down some years ago, and lighting and navigation lights were installed in 1997 along with a new shelter in 1999.

Shandon had a different type of pier, built in 1886 with criss-cross iron and timber supports. The Free Church stood guard at the landward end but it has now become residential. The pier closed to steamers in 1915 but only disappeared without trace when the road was widened in 1969.

In July 1933, Clyde Flying Boats Ltd offered pleasure flights at 10/- and longer trips to see Loch Lomond for £1. Similar flights from Glasgow now cost £120! The seaplane belonged to Tom Guthrie, son of Sir James Guthrie, a 'Glasgow Boy' artist.

Whether the quality of sea water or the heat of the summer has changed, it seems unlikely that pony rides will again be offered on Helensburgh's beach. Janice Gentles enjoys this treat with her father Jim in 1953.

It also seems unlikely that the many day-trippers to the town will now take to the waters in such numbers, although it is possible, as anyone will see if they greet an electric train from Glasgow on a Holiday Monday morning in a heat wave!

A period picture of recreation between the pier and the old parish church, c.1900. A travelling fair with helter-skelter, swings and roundabout is next to the permanent bandstand. All the ladies wear ankle-length skirts and two policemen stand in West Clyde Street but do not seem to be needed.

The Glasgow, Dumbarton & Helensburgh Railway reached Helensburgh in 1857, but the station was at George Street. By 1862 it had been brought to East Princes Street to the east of the present Central Station, as shown in this 1875 picture. In 1877 the Council required the station to be built in its present position, and was relieved to hear that the Company no longer wished to take the tracks to the pier in the face of public opinion that it would 'arrest the progress and destroy the prospects of the town'. One of the large stone gateposts is all that survives and it still shows where part had to be cut to allow a goods line to cross East Princes Street to the Gas Works.

The Upper Station on Sinclair Street, at a height of 220ft above sea level. In 1976 its typical West Highland Railway 'chalet' buildings and double track were in place and being served by a diesel-electric locomotive. Although the building and up loop line has gone, there is a substantial traffic to Fort William, Mallaig and Oban from Glasgow.

At Central Station in 1955, Gresley V1 Class locomotive No. 67619 has been cleaned and prepared for the 8.26 a.m. express run to Glasgow by Fireman Bobbie Brodie for Driver Willie Rae. Note the polished brass work and gleaming boiler casing and compare with the 8.15 a.m. stopping loco! It is also interesting to see the glazed canopy over the platforms.

There used to be an engine shed next to the station, where several locomotives were kept and prepared for working the Glasgow and the West Highland lines. Driver Jimmy Redmond is standing by the turntable and the buildings that replaced Alma Place are prominent.

RAILWAY TEMPERANCE HOTEL,
HELENSBURGH.

MRS. BEWLEY - Proprietrix.
CHEAP WEEK-END TARIFF.

The Railway Temperance Hotel in East Princes Street was opposite the Central Railway Station. Mrs Bewley, proprietrix, offered a cheap weekend tariff in 1910. On the street level, M. McPhee was a wine and spirit merchant and provided a restaurant. The name board can still be seen though painted out and the ground floor is now an empty shop and The Station Bar!

Whilst the bicycle was well established by 1899, it would also obviously be the most convenient form of transport and recreation in the town. Here, Ralph and Archie Templeton stand by their upright roadster cycles, but just look at the formality of the clothing!

'Cairndhu' was designed in 1872 by architect William Leiper for the Provost of Glasgow, Lord Strathclyde. Later another Lord Provost, Sir John Ure, lived there. It was a hotel at the time of this cheerful picture of four chefs, but closed abruptly in 1984. Currently it is the Cairndhu House Nursing Home and the white name picked out in its grassy embankment is a local landmark.

Craigendoran Pier opened in 1892 and closed to passengers in 1973. Final fitting out of an oil exploration rig in 1974 for the Marathon (formerly John Brown) Yard at Clydebank may have been one of its more unusual activities. The height of the jacking legs required that the rig pass under Erskine Bridge before final fitting.

Waldie & Co. were motor and carriage engineers in Sinclair Street, with an entrance under the buildings where Intersport are now. This early 1920s picture shows the staff outing preparing to depart on a four-horse carriage. No fewer than eighteen men plus the coachman are on board, and the proprietor is seeing them off.

Captain Jack Wylie was so proud of his RAMC staff car in May 1918. He is believed to have settled in New Zealand after the war.

Gareloch Motor Service Co. Ltd used the Old Granary buildings as a depot. They operated public transport to Clynder, Garelochhead and Kilcreggan with uniformed drivers.

Watts Yard Motor House & Repair Shop at 53 and 86 Sinclair Street was in the country!

The first advertisement for *The Comet*, a steamboat service from Glasgow, to Greenock and thence to Helensburgh, appeared on 5 August 1812 above the signature of Henry Bell of the Baths Inn. On 11 March 1833, James Clelland in a letter to the Editor of the *Glasgow Herald* wrote: 'It is a remarkable fact that in January 1812 when Henry Bell launched his small steamer *Comet*, of three horsepower, on the Clyde at Glasgow, there was not a steam vessel in Europe, and that at the expiry of twenty-one years, there are on the same river seventy-three steamers.'

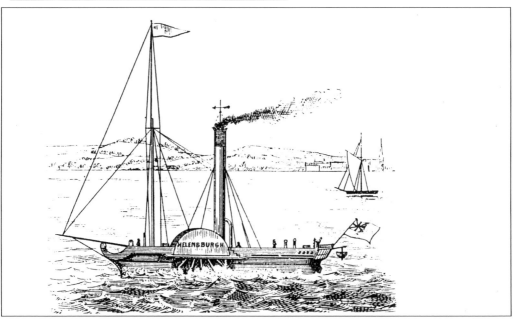

One of them was *Helensburgh*, a paddle steamer built in 1825 for the Glasgow, Helensburgh and Roseneath Steamboat Company. It was the first to be fitted with an iron mast and plied the Clyde until 1835. In 1827, under Captain John Turner, *Helensburgh* came second in the Northern Yacht Club regatta from Rothesay Bay to Greater Cumbrae and back. She was sold in 1835 to become a Mersey ferry for a further ten years and was broken up in 1845. It is thought that no other boat has sported the town name.

Four
Growing and Relaxing

On the left is Robert Hodge Sinclair and a friend in full dress, perhaps for a wedding. He was a chemist in John Street. This studio portrait was by R. Todd at 148 West Princes Street.

Grant Street Public School was built by private subscription in 1853 following a campaign by the Revd John Bell (*d.*1896) of the Episcopal Church, though whether it provided the service he wished for is not now clear. It was demolished in 1876 to make way for the gasworks and was known locally as the 'Ragged Industrial School', probably because it catered particularly for children of the poorest families. Two brothers are said to be examining a penny given them by grocer Dow. By 1930 the barefoot boy, James Loan, had a motor hire and garage business in the town.

This is perhaps the most ecumenical and versatile building to have existed in the town! Row School Board built it in 1890 for infants and primary school but made it redundant on the opening of their Clyde Street School in 1904. St Michael's Episcopal church took over and used it as a denominational school until 1913 when it reverted to the School Board and was attended by infants until 1933. Next, St Joseph's Roman Catholic Church acquired it as a primary school, extending it in 1935 and 1959, and finally, demolition came in 1980 to enable the building of Waverley Court sheltered housing scheme. Only the front railings in West King and James Streets survive.

The first Hermitage School was built in East Argyle Street in 1875, on land formerly part of Hermitage House that was made available by the Cramb family. The Architect was William Spence of 'Ardlui', 23 Charlotte Street, who also designed both the St Columba and Rhu churches. However, this building was demolished in 1967 in favour of a much larger, replacement building at Colgrain. As in other schools, the stonework proclaimed the 'School Board of Row.' The art room is on the far right, science in the centre, and the headmaster's room on the first floor of the centre tower.

The Clyde Industrial Training Ship *Empress* was anchored off Rhu Bay from 1889-1923, where many thousands of boys were prepared for service in the Merchant or Royal Navy. The ship (then named *Revenge*) had seen service in the Baltic from 1854-1856 in the Crimean War, and retired to the Gare Loch in 1890. *Empress* was a replacement for the *Cumberland*, which had had the same duties from 1869, but had been destroyed by a fire, possibly started by the ships' company! The boys' band often performed in the town bandstands.

The senior pupils of St Bride's School in 1906. From left to right, back row: Betty Paterson, Nance Anderson, Amy Ross. Middle row: Madge Gillespie, Margaret Campbell, Stana Brett, Hanna Leiper, H. McPhee. Front row: Noel Nicholl, Winnie Hunt, Madge MacCrossan, Hetttie Smith. The High School for Girls was founded in 1895 but by 1903 had been re-named St Bride's and it continued as an independent girls school until 1977. William Anderson was one of the founding directors.

Hermitage school concert in 1950. The fourth, fifth and sixth years are performing.

Hermitage School staff in the early 1950s. The front row are from left to right: Miss Howison, Dr Simpson, Miss Robertson, headmaster Mr George Mutch, Miss Leny, Mr Gray, Miss Kemp and, top right, janitor Thomas Dunlop.

Walking in 1934-1935. In front of the Bank of Scotland, then at No.36 West Clyde Street, is Mrs Alexander Gentles with her schoolboy sons, Jim (carrying his Mother's basket), and Jack, probably on their way to the family butchers business.

Larchfield School photograph in Summer Term 1955. St Bride's Girls School merged with Larchfield in 1977 to form Lomond School, but their separate origins as privately run schools may go back as far as 1850. Following a fire in February 1997 in St Bride's building, which facilitated a rebuild, Larchfield building was declared redundant and sold for residential development.

John Logie Baird was a pupil at Larchfield School in 1900, and is shown in his school uniform.

Another pupil was his friend Jack Buchanan, who would have been ten when JLB took this photograph. Later in life Jack became famous as an international entertainer and film star.

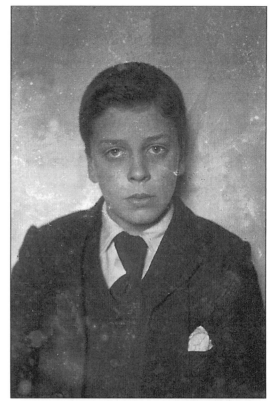

At the early age of twelve, in 1900, John Logie Baird was experimenting with timed photography and even took his own picture in bed! Note the skeleton and face behind the bed head.

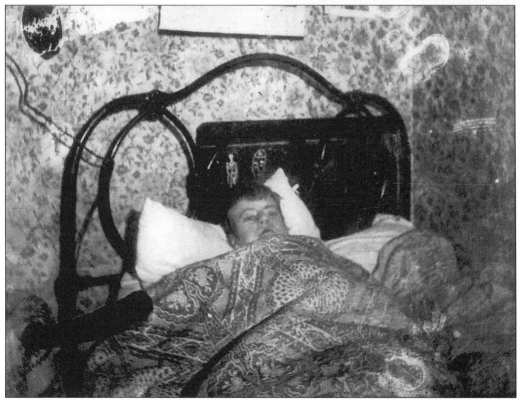

A game of putting on the lawns in front of Drumgarve, John Street in 1894. The five unmarried Templeton sisters in formal dress are taking the final putt very seriously. They were all interested in the suffrage movement and would have been described as 'modern women.'

Miss W. Wedgwood receiving the Helensburgh and District Badminton Club's Ladies Championship Vase from Mrs D.J. Dunbar of Old Kilpatrick at the Drill Hall, probably in 1935-1936. From left to right are: Nora Smellie, Isabel Clyde, Mrs Dunbar, Jenny Gillon, Winnie Slater (Womens Doubles), Winifred Wedgwood, Dot Carson, Rob Paterson (Tournament Secretary), Donald Cameron, Geddes Troup, Iris Snodgrass and Graeme Cooper.

A tennis party in the 1880s on the lawns at 'Drumgarve', (now the site of Drumgarve Court).
Relaxation in the gardens of the Helensburgh villas was a popular subject with both artists and
photographers. In 1885 Sir John Lavery painted *The Tennis Party* which was considered a major
achievement by one of 'The Glasgow Boys.'

Helensburgh and Gareloch Horticultural Society was founded in 1850 and has been very successful in combining the talents and resources of the professional gardeners, owners and flower lovers of the area. The Honourable Commander A.D. Cochrane DSO, MP, conducted the opening ceremony for the 71st Annual Flower Show in 1932. The prizewinners did not look very happy at having their photograph taken! From left to right: A. Goodlet (who owned a slaughterhouse in Grant Street), J.G. Burgess (painter and decorator), W. Barratt, P. Bauchop and A. Borthwick.

Members of 'The Tin House Club' which formed in 1932. George R. Murray presented a medal for an annual competition among those golfers who had been members when the Helensburgh Golf Clubhouse was made of wood and corrugated iron! From left to right, back row: W.K. Maclachlan, A. McDougall (vet), R.C. Lindsay (auctioneer), R. Stanton (lawyer), W. Easton (grocer), -?-. Front row: A. McCulloch (decorater), A. Douglas (coal businessman), R. Ness (lawyer) G.R. Murray, A. Stewart, W. Ferguson, T. Turnbull (golf professional).

Helensburgh Golf Club was founded in 1893 and the tin hut was built near to the Old Luss Road in the following year at a cost of £295. Two members, with their caddies, tee off from the original first hole.

Nance Anderson with a group of Cub Scouts – this is unusual as she was renowned for her work with the Guides and Brownies!

Dr Janet M.S. Glen, then Captain of the 2nd Helensburgh Girl Guide company in their 1968 photograph. Among others, featured in this photograph are: Aileen McKinnon, Susan Buck, Cindy Pledger, Gillian Dunlop, Mary Dutch, Lucy Roberts, Jane Day, Zoe Roberts, Jean Carter, Hazel Stewart, Anne Hardie, Tina Henderson, Elizabeth Walker, Irene Stark, Anne Day, Julie De'Ath, Sheena Smith and Sheila Lawson.

From an earlier period, the 4th Helensburgh Troop of Girl Guides in 1925/26. Note the hats, solid uniforms and stern expressions, perhaps caused by a long film exposure. From left to right, back row: N. Allan, D. Aird, M. McMillan, M. Wilson, M. Laing, C. Haldane, S. Smith, -?-, -?-, N. Graham. Third row: C. Martin, A. Kennedy, I. Paton, C. Paton, C. Fraser, B. Fair, L. Robertson, B. Wilson, M. Rae, I. Wilson, I. Green. Second row: A. Dallady, E. Martin, M. Gray, H. Forsyth, I. Green, P. Bathgate, -?-, M. Bain, I. Ferguson, N. Tier. Front row: A. Baillie, M. Stevenson, N. Thomson, M. Scott, -?-, M. McDonald, L. Paton.

Miss Rankine (?) makes the 1942 collection for Red Cross funds in East Clyde Street, and is supported by Angela McCulloch in her Junior Red Cross outfit.

Although many individual athletes from Helensburgh have reached the top in their sport, not often have teams done the same. In 1967 the Scottish Amateur Cup was won by Rhu Amateurs Football Club, founded in 1866. Celebrations were in order!

Hermitage Former Pupils Football Club, season of 1912/13. From left to right, back row: S. Carson, R. Duncan, R. Martin, J. MacFarlane, W. Buchanan, T. White, J.Gilmour. Front row: ? Morrison, S. Brown, W. Roxborough, W. Wright, G. McLachlan, A. McCulloch, F. Duncan, T. McFarquhar. This club was revived after the Second World War and offered several sports for a number of years.

Craighelen Lawn Tennis Club in 1928. Among this happy group are Mary Cooper, Walter Bryden and his wife, and Jimmy Miller.

Helensburgh Operatic Society presented *Magyar Melody* in its thirtieth season in March 1956. From left to right are: Joan Gillespie and John Miller, Jimmy Nicol and Pat Orr, Jimmy White and Margaret Wapinshaw, Jimmy Sloss and Irene Armstrong, Jimmy Swankie and Elspeth Cameron, and Jim McColl and Ruby Gentles. Jim is now well known in *The Beechgrove Garden* on television.

A paddling pool existed on the foreshore for a number of years and was refilled twice daily by the incoming tide!

The first motor car bought by Nance Anderson was a Wolseley Coupé. Note the circular petrol tank mounted on the back and the spare can on the running board. 'Joe' the dog stands guard.

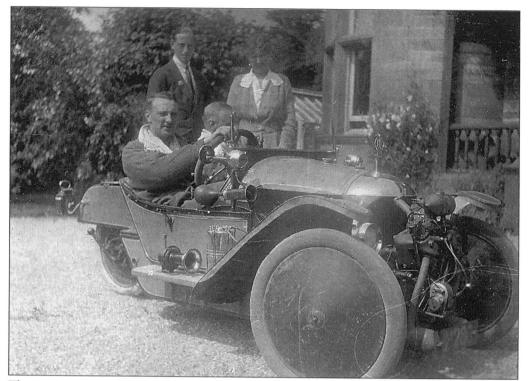

The area was very keen on early motor cars. In August 1917 Kenneth Anderson drove a Morgan three-wheeler (the car with its moving parts out in front). His brother John is seated, while his sister Frank is standing. Nance took the photograph.

Helensburgh West Beach.

Back to the seaside, or rather the beach, for a long view of a sandcastle building competition. There appear to be at least twenty teams competing in the pegged out areas, but maybe it is an individual effort because there seem to be forty white labels on the plots.

A full view in 1968 of the outdoor swimming pool and, beyond, across the Firth to Greenock. This pool only survived for about a year after the opening of the adjacent indoor pool in 1977. Clearance, however, was delayed for a long time and it only disappeared into a children's play area as part of an upgrade of the promenade in 1996.

Curling, ice hockey and skating at the top of Sinclair Street in 1969. Previous curling and skating ponds had existed at East King Street, corner of Henry Bell Street, and at Havelock Street. Both ponds were much nearer to sea level and, therefore, less easily frozen in winter. The sites were redeveloped for housing, but the present one now seems secure and was upgraded in 1997 as an environmental improvement to await the return of cold winters.

Five
Glen Fruin

Glen Fruin was, and still is, a fertile rural valley within immediate reach of the town. Well-scattered occasional farms and cottages border the Fruin Water flowing through the Glen to empty into Loch Lomond at Mid Ross. The one-teacher school was built in 1840 and appears from this picture taken around 1910 to have only had two pupils. The spread of education is seen from the equal size of the maps, one of Scotland and the other of England and Wales. Musical scales and a 'Great Colouring Competition' sponsored by Carrs Rich Tea Biscuits decorate the timber walls.

The country road from Cross Keys to Faslane may always have been extremely quiet. In 1910 Robert Thorburn of Helensburgh captured this photograph of a pony and trap carrying three men at speed along an isolated straight stretch.

However, a traffic jam could be caused by grazing ponies! A different carriage and single young driver await the pleasure of seven ponies while two cows watch over the fence. The view is from West Kilbride Farm with Auchenvennel Hill on the left and Beinn Tharsuinn on the right.

In another part of the glen, Mother shows a boy and girl how to pick wild flowers in a meadow behind the farm. No longer do such meadows grow and it is now against the law to pick any wild flowers that do manage to thrive.

This superb picture of a lone skater on the frozen Fruin Water is another of the series by Robert Thorburn taken between 1908 and 1912. How reminiscent of the famous painting by Sir Henry Raeburn of *The Reverend Robert Walker Skating on Duddingston Loch*!

A charming scene, again from around 1910, of two children in the dress of the period climbing on a six-barred gate leaning against a dry stane wall and three-rail fence. Presumably the gate, seen here loose, would be lashed across the lane to divert the cattle at milking time.

Of the five cows in the foreground, at least three are Highland cattle. The trees are atop an early Bronze Age burial mound.

Another gate to a farm with, perhaps, the farmer inviting the camera in. This and the previous pictures were discovered and used in a calendar for 1978 that was published in a limited edition by the Admiralty Marine Technology Establishment sited at the west end of the glen. The original negative plates were loaned by local artist Gregor Ian Smith (1907-1985) who lived in the Old School House from the 1950s. He was President and Trustee of the Helensburgh and District Art Club and his work is represented in the Anderson Trust Collection of Paintings.

The Fruin Water spread into pools and provided summer recreation and picnic areas. Two ladies from the Anderson family paddle in June 1919.

A group of scientists from the French company Dassault on a 1964 visit with, on the right, James Norman, the superintendent of the Admiralty Hydroballistic Research Establishment. They were interested in measures to facilitate the escape of aircrew from any 'ditched' carrier-borne aircraft. Martin Baker, who had refined ejector seats, was also using the Glen Fruin test tank for practical tests on naval aircraft. The tank, 150ft long, 30ft wide and 45ft deep, with 166 armour-plated windows and powerful lights, allowed full vision and photography. Most of the world's air forces now use the ejector equipment.

The AHR Establishment, covered in snow. The tank was built to test rocket launching in clear filtered water. Post-war, there was a wave-maker and a slamming rig to test impact pressures on ship hull sections at full scale. The facility closed in 1988 and became an Army training camp.

Quiet as the Glen has been portrayed, on 7 February 1603 there was a substantial battle when Clan Colquhoun and Clan Gregor fought the Battle of Glen Fruin. At least 140 Colquhouns and two MacGregors were killed. Later, twenty-five MacGregors were executed and all were declared outlaws, their lands on the east side of Loch Lomond being forfeited to the Crown.

Helensburgh Heritage Trust promoted the restoration of the Battle Memorial Stone, originally placed by Robert Arbuthnott, Lord Lieutenant of the County. On 11 October 1997, this handshake at the unveiling ceremony between representatives of the formerly warring clans may have been the first for nearly 400 years – and at the largest public gathering in the glen for a very, very long time. Shaking hands are Nial Colquhoun (left) and Iain MacGregor representing their Clan Chieftains, while behind them, holding the flag, are H. Stewart Noble, Chairman of the Heritage Trust (left), and Councillor William Petrie, Argyll & Bute Council and the Regional Tourist Board. Pipe Major John Low of Helensburgh and District Pipe Band provides the soundtrack.

Six
War Times

Rosa Isobel Templeton (1868-1936), working with the war wounded at Hermitage House Auxiliary Military Hospital in 1917. Her early life was in British Guiana but she lived for many years at 'Drumgarve', John Street, and became an acclaimed watercolour artist.

The Clyde Royal Garrison Artillery 2/2 Company marching on the Shandon Road in 1915. Two pipers lead the march as small children run alongside. The *Lucy Ashton*, as ever, lies at Garelochhead Pier. Few photographs of the Gareloch exist without showing this workhorse of the loch on her twice daily rounds.

The Templeton/Anderson family mounted pictures of their serving contributors to the war effort on the wall of their entrance hall at Inistore, John Street.

Supplement to The Post Sunday Special, Nov. 28th. 1915.

PATRIOTIC HELENSBURGH FAMILY.

A patriotic Helensburgh Family. This postcard was issued on 28 November 1915 as one of a series of supplements to the *Sunday Post*. It shows father and mother Mr and Mrs James Nicholson, their six sons, and two grandsons serving in the forces. From left to right, back row: Mr James Nicholson, Mrs Nicholson, Sgt Archie Nicholson RSF, Pte Alex Nicholson, Gunner Donald Nicholson RFA. Front row: Pte James Nicholson A&SH, Pte James Nicholson, A&SH (Grandson), Pte Robert Nicholson, A&SH (Grandson), Pte Roderick Nicholson (Dead), Gunner Duncan Nicholson, RFA.

Another view of the Garrison Company on the march, returning along the Road at Rhu with Kenneth and John Anderson setting the pace.

In convalescence, the war wounded were able to use the facilities of Helensburgh Bowling Club in East Abercromby Street. They wore blue suits with red ties and are seen here on the Bowling Green with members of the club, which had been established in 1861. In more recent times a member of the pop group Wet Wet Wet had the house seen in the background.

As well as a war, the area suffered a potato famine – or at any rate the people of Greenock sent their children over the water to Helensburgh to seek supplies. The photos were published under the title 'Helensburgh Invaded'. The incursion seems to have been successful!

A first aid demonstration, or perhaps examination, by the Helensburgh (North British Railway) Section of the Red Cross on a platform of Central Station.

The horse-drawn ambulance which attended the event belonged to the Victoria Infirmary.

The Second World War also affected the town – initially by the excavation of an air raid shelter in the putting green and grass on the seafront. That it may never have been used was more to do with the ingress of sea water than any lack of enemy activity!

During wartime, there were strict restrictions on photography and we believe that this is why no pictures from 1939-1945 have been offered for publication. To suggest the period this view across the Gareloch in late 1949 shows the liner *Aquitania* waiting for the breakers yard, H.M.S. *Defence*, *Pioneer* and *Scylla* as well as the *Campania* which had been converted into an exhibition ship in readiness for the Festival of Britain held in 1951.

In the post-war period, military rocket development took place in the Outer Hebrides. Servicing of the Benbecula Rocket Range was undertaken from Helensburgh Pier. In 1959 three vessels are moored abreast, but disturbance was caused in the town by their generators and eventually the service moved to the hangars at Rhu.

A second view of the service vessels, contrasted with summer sunbathers on the Esplanade, and many, many bathers in the sea. Apparently, in weather like this, the crews played cricket on the decks resulting in very strange sounds from the cargo area!

A memorial to those who died in the First World War was erected in front of Shandon Church. This is the 1978 Remembrance Day Service with The Rev. David Stirling. When the church closed in 1981 the memorial was stored, but a campaign resulted in its re-erection in 1987 in a garden on the main road. A plaque recording the names of those who died in 1939-1945 was added in 1994.

To mark the end of the war at 11 a.m. on the 11th day of the 11th month of 1918, victory parades were organised when Soldiers returned. The Civic Party are standing on a draped wagon outside St.Andrew's Kirk (now West Kirk) whilst the troops stand 'at ease' and the pipe band plays. Crowds of townspeople surround the north-east quadrant of Colquhoun Square.

Seven
Faslane Port

The K class submarines were the Royal Navy's first attempt to build a submarine fast enough to keep up with the Fleet and were powered by steam turbines when on the surface. On 29 January 1917 the K13 was in the Gareloch on trials from Fairfields, Govan, when the boiler room flooded and she sank. The captain and forty-eight men escaped from the forward section after fifty-four hours but twenty-nine crew and shipyard workers drowned. After six weeks the craft was raised, refitted and was in service until 1926, though then renumbered K22. A Memorial in Faslane Cemetery is the scene of an annual service of remembrance.

Dating from 1937, or thereabouts, here is an indication of the scale of the West Highland Branch railway line and yard behind the berthing area – and the start of building works for both a port and a shipbreakers yard.

Early traffic at Military Port No.1 in 1942. Aeroplanes on the quayside await loading on a carrier.

The Royal Navy organised a Family Day in 1959 to enable relatives of employees and servicemen to visit and see for themselves. The public were also admitted. This picture shows that 'just a few' people wanted to stand on two submarines and go down the hatch!

In August 1955 the submarine 'mother ship' *Adamant* moved from Rothesay to Faslane with four submarines alongside.

A view extending from the Oil Terminal in the far distance, with the deep water berths on the right, to the Admiralty Floating Dock No.60 in 1960. Submarines can be seen alongside but there is not a lot of activity at the time of the photograph.

Unique to the Royal Navy, the shiplift at HM Naval Base Clyde is capable of lifting the largest submarines clear of the water. It is seen here at night with a view of the interior, where a submarine is undergoing a service. In 1998 HM Naval Base Clyde was one of the largest employers in Scotland with a budget of £160 million and staff of 3,450 civilians and 1,000 from the Royal Navy. Two thousand service personnel make up the crews from the ships and submarines.

An exercise between a Vanguard-class submarine and a helicopter of 819 Squadron from HMS *Gannet* at Prestwick. Presumably a crew member is to be winched up or down, so the helicopter will not be landing on the missile tubes!

An alternative view of the base from above Garelochhead, showing the helicopter landing pad, the shiplift, submarine berths and the 'floating dock' in 1995. In the far distance are Rhu Narrows which have to be navigated by all ships entering the Gareloch.

An aerial view of the base. The diversion of the main road round the base can be seen and the 'floating dock' is in position in the foreground but its replacement, the shiplift, is under construction in the centre. This extensive view shows Gareloch in front and, over the hill, Loch Long. In the extreme left distance is the entrance to Loch Goil with snow covered hills. The development of the sites at Faslane and Coulport had taken eight years and cost £1.7 billion – regarded as one of the largest construction projects in Europe.

HMS *Vanguard*, the first of the Vanguard Class, arriving in October 1992 for Contractors Sea Trials at Faslane. She is passing through Rhu Narrows, which had been specially dredged to allow passage of these very large craft, with her escort from the base. There are many escorting naval vessels.

A peace camp was established on Ministry of Defence land on 12 June 1982 but subsequently moved 500 yards to the roadside verge of the A814. In the background is Shandon House, used for some years as a residential school but now owned by the Ministry of Defence.

The camp developed, personnel changed and trees and scrub grew up around it, somewhat lessening the environmental impact. The Strathclyde Regional and Dumbarton District councils gave some support. Argyll & Bute Council, however, is less supportive and has the legal right to recover its land but faces considerable physical problems. In 1999 it is reported that one of the psychedelic caravans, in use for over fifteen years, is displayed at Glasgow Museum of Transport. A spokeswoman is reported as saying 'it will engage the hearts and minds of our visitors – it is certainly very topical and relevant in today's society.'

The Wilkinson Sword of Peace was awarded to HMS *Neptune*, Clyde, on 23 October 1991 in recognition of outstanding effort by the unit in fostering good relations in the area. Since 1966, Wilkinson Sword Ltd has sponsored this special award, for presentation annually to a unit selected by the Ministry of Defence on the recommendation of the Admiralty, Army and RAF Boards. At the Main Gate, the Sword, which is standard service pattern, is displayed beneath the Honours Board of actions undertaken by successive HMS *Neptune* vessels. The current *Neptune* is a 'stone frigate' – a building within the base!

The Wilkinson Sword of Peace, where it hangs below HMS *Neptune*'s Honours Board.

A visit to the Clyde by the Royal Yacht *Britannia* on 10 May 1968, bringing HM Queen Elizabeth the Queen Mother for the commissioning of the submarine base. Commodore D.G. Kent escorts.

HRH Prince Andrew, a serving naval officer, visits the base in October 1994 on account of the decommissioning of HMS *Resolution*, which had been in service for twenty-seven years.

The Right Honourable John Major, the Prime Minister, visited on 28 August 1996 for the decommissioning of HMS *Repulse* at the end of the Polaris deterrent era, which had lasted from June 1968 and had involved 229 submarine patrols.

The training ship *Royalist* pays a visit to HMS *Neptune* in September 1995, representing the traditions and service of the Royal Navy.

Diana, Princess of Wales is shown in October 1986 looking through the periscope of HMS *Trafalgar* at the Firth of Clyde. The vessel had returned from Brest, and the Princess, who had been hoisted on board in the Firth of Clyde, was taken for a dive before being returned to shore by tender. Commander Toby Elliot offers guidance.

Eight
Happenings

At 9 a.m. on the morning of Friday 9 August 1974, Her Majesty's Royal Yacht *Britannia* was saluted in the Gareloch by 110 yachts in a formation of five columns. They were led by the John Dunlop Urie, DL, Commodore of the Royal Northern Yacht Club and were on time to salute Her Majesty, patron of the club - thus commencing celebrations of the 150th anniversary of the club.

After arriving at Faslane the royal party returned to club headquarters at Rhu to be greeted on the lawns by 500 guests. A plaque was presented and royal portraits autographed. Her Majesty and Prince Philip walk the shore path and inspect the Sea Scouts' Guard of Honour.

For the return to Faslane the royal party embarked on the royal barge at the club pier. The Queen and Duke of Edinburgh held a reception on board *Britannia* at Clyde Submarine Base, Faslane, that evening. The escort is Commodore Urie.

The Duke (1845-1914) and Duchess (Princess Louise 1848-1939) of Argyll are received on Helensburgh Pier around 1910. They are welcomed by the provost and, on the left, the town clerks. At this time there were joint town clerks, George McLachlan (*b*.1823) and his son John Butt McLachlan (*b*.1855). A considerable naval guard of honour is lined up.

Prime Minister Stanley Baldwin about to lay a wreath at the War Memorial on 15 June 1928. From left to right: Baillie Archie C. Robb, Baillie John Muir, Provost Ronald R. Herbertson, the Prime Minister and Sir Iain Colquhoun (Lord Lieutenant of Dunbartonshire). The visit was primarily to unveil a stained glass window in St Andrews church (now West Kirk) dedicated to the memory of his predecessor as Prime Minister in 1922, the Right Honourable Andrew Bonar Law. Bonar Law had been brought up in the town by his cousins, the Kidston family, and had been an elder of West Kirk who had also taught in the Sunday School.

At appropriate intervals the Clyde celebrates the achievement of Henry Bell and *The Comet*. Provost J. McLeod Williamson fully entered into the spirit of the 150th anniversary and arrived at the Pier in period dress carrying an umbrella reputed to have belonged to Henry Bell!

For the same anniversary, in 1962, Sir William Lithgow sponsored the construction of a working replica of *The Comet*. On 18 September, as part of a special regatta, she is seen approaching Helensburgh Pier escorted by yachts returning from the General Handicap Race for members of the Helensburgh Sailing Club.

From time to time Helensburgh suffers from severe weather. The west bay catches south-westerly winds from far down the Firth of Clyde and a coincidence of high tides with gale force winds can result in severe flooding. In 1922 the rough seas, all but engulfing the pier, were caught on camera and published as a postcard.

Hurricane 'Debbie' arrived on Saturday 16 September 1961 from the American coast, having been described as a spent force. By 3 p.m. waves were breaking over the sea front in great curtains of spray. At 4 p.m. Craigendoran and Helensburgh Piers were awash and sailing craft were being torn from their moorings and thrown ashore. The height of the fury was at 5 p.m. and trees were soon uprooted inland. Incidents were still being reported to the police the next day.

Not the effect of 'Debbie', nor the severe gale which hit the town in January 1968, this yacht was washed ashore in the Gareloch by strong winds and high seas in the summer of that year.

The Royal National Lifeboat Institution established a Lifeboat Station at Rhu in 1965. A 16ft D Class boat served until 1978 when an Atlantic 21 took over the area, covering the water from Glasgow to Dunoon, including four sea lochs and 200 miles of coastline. Originally this prefabricated garage was the boathouse, but a new building with full facilities for the volunteer crews was opened in August 1997. Pictured in the 1983 crew and officials were, from left to right: Ferdi Thurgood, Mike Roberts, George Newlands, Graeme Busby, Peter Macneill, Colin Gardiner, Mike Hutchinson, George Hulley, Alan Wallace, Paul Fenning, James Robertson, Jim Potts, the late George Gardiner, John Gorrie and the late George Gray. The present lifefboat was gifted in 1990 and has GPS navigation, 70hp twin engines, is manned by three crew, and continues the tradition which has seen 1,000 launches and the rescue of 226 lives.

Two motor cars collided on 4 June 1906 at the junction of Glasgow and West Princes Streets. Instead of collapsing, one turned over and the other ended up on its side. The vehicle on the right belonged to Mr Kirkpatrick of Lagbuie, Shandon and the other to Mr F. McAlpine of Helensburgh.

Davie Wilson ran this car as a bus from helensburgh to Rhu, and occasionally ended up on the beach at Kidston! It was of sufficient importance, however, to be published as a postcard!

The 1898 undertakers for the funeral of D. G. McCallum were J. & R. Grant, and the cost of best hearse and pair (of black horses) with attendants was £5, but this was not an economy ceremony. Note the discount of 2s.

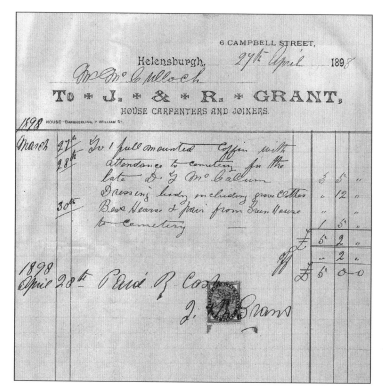

The funeral procession of an English postman who had transferred to Helensburgh in the interests of his health but, unfortunately, did not survive for long. The cortège passes the head post office towards the sea front and is followed by uniformed colleagues and at least two more carriages. The numbers suggest that perhaps the deceased had been head postmaster.

Arms and the Man was produced by Nance Anderson at the Victoria Hall in March 1922. The cast of this well dressed production are from left to right: Rex Clapperton, Captain Watson, Betty Paterson, Mr Barrie, Isabel Ram, Laurence Paul, Penelope Kidston and R.T. Templeton.

Forms Two and Three of St Bride's presented scenes from *The Young Visiters* or *Mr Salteena's Plan* by Miss Daisy Ashford, in the School Hall on 25-26 June 1920. A total of £20 was raised for the Dr Elsie Inglis Memorial Fund, which supported Scottish Womens Hospitals, particularly in Serbia. Among the costumed characters are Catherine Rodger, Ursula Butler, Margaret MacGregor, Esther Melling, Katharine Frew, Jean Anderson and Mary Walker. Production was by Nance Anderson.

A Fancy Dress Ball was held at the Victoria Hall in January 1920. From left to right, back row: Charlie Martin, Dr Downes, Captain Watson, Nance Anderson, E. Hobson, Betty Patterson, Laurence Paul, Colin Penn, Dick Kidston, Major Purvis and Rex Clapperton. Middle Row: R.T. Templeton, Mrs Strang, Ethel Cuthbert, Hilda Hamilton, Mrs Watson, Frank, May Young, Sybil Henderson. Front Row: Fraser Campbell, Mr Strang, Vi Paterson, Penelope Paul, Mrs Martin, Isobel Penn, Mrs E. Raeburn, Tom Guthrie and, reclining in front, John Anderson.

The Arts League of Service Travelling Theatre from London visited in 1922. Among the cast was Donald Wolfit (later knighted and one of the great actor-managers), and Nance Anderson organised the hospitality. Touring theatre and opera groups still often visit the town.

To mark the centenary of the West Highland Railway in 1994, Helensburgh Community Council chartered a Sprinter Train for a week and recreated the 'Wee Arrochar', a train which served area commuters for many years. Twice-daily excursions from Helensburgh Central to Arrochar and Tarbet station were sold out. The Colgrain Dancers performed here in the Central Station concourse and the Margaret Rose Dancers greeted passengers on the forecourt at Tarbet.

The West Highland Railway Company's 100 miles of track from Craigendoran to Fort William was opened on 11 August 1894 and was the longest length of railway ever opened on one day. Helensburgh Community Council coordinated the Centenary Celebrations in 1994. On 7 August a double-headed steam train from Glasgow to Fort William marked the actual day. At the Upper Station from left to right: George Gray, Trevor Welch, Dumbarton Provost Pat O'Neill, Alan A.R. Day (Chairman of the organising committee), and passengers.

At Platform One of Central Station, the 'Wee Arrochar' sprinter unit, billboard and passengers await the 2 p.m. departure.

A view of the double-headed steam special arriving at the Upper Station. K4 No.3442, *The Great Marquess*, leads K1 No. 2005 hauling a packed train. The 'bus shelter' waiting room replacing the chalet station building has since been removed, but there is increasing rail traffic on the line.

Helensburgh Outdoor Swimming Pool was the gift of Baillie Andrew Buchanan in 1928. In 1937 the young bathers are happily splashing – but they may also have been shivering!

For many years, 8 a.m. on Ne'erday (1 January) has seen considerable numbers of volunteers participate in a short swim in the sea, originally from Helensburgh Pier, but recently from Rhu Marina where there are facilities and the LifeboatStation. On 1 January 1982 these hardy souls leapt into the sea from the Pier.

From the old end-of-pier building, shivering bathers leave the changing rooms in 1967.

In the water at the start of 1960, these swimmers are under supervision from a row boat beside the pier.

Another pier event was the departure in 1911 of Mr Tommy Sang for a new life in New York. The collection of be-hatted men and boys gathered for the send off, with accompanying piper.

After fifty years service Tom Turnbull retired in 1945 from his role as golf professional at Helensburgh Golf Club. Committee and members posed for this formal picture. From left to right, back row: Messrs McCulloch, Aitkenhead, Easton, Keir, Davidson. Third row: Messrs McAuley, Clements, Herbeson, Spy. Second row: Messrs Michie, McAuslan, Jack, Douglas. Front row: Messers Colville, Rafferty, Workman, Downs, Fairbairn. Front row, centre: Mr Tom Turnbull.

To mark the Coronation in 1953 flowering cherry trees were planted by schools. This is the planting party from Larchfield at the south-eastern corner of Stafford and James Streets. From the left the young planters were Stewart Sandeman, Stewart Noble (now Heritage Trust Chairman), Alexander Kennedy, William Marshall and a helper, probably from the Burgh Parks Department.

British Columbia Fruit Growers in Canada, in around 1951, donated apples which were ceremonially distributed to school children. Miss Lennie hands them out at the primary school, with Miss May Henderson and Miss McPherson controlling.

Following the wedding in 1926 of Arthur McCulloch and Janice Kirkwood at St Columba Church, this photograph was taken at their reception at Shandon Hydro. The two mothers, Mrs D. McCulloch and Mrs Kirkwood are seated on the front row. Miss M. Kirkwood, Mr R. Spy and Miss T. Coutts are in the centre of the back row. Revd J. Walker 0is at the right – he had been first club champion of Helensburgh Golf Club in 1924. Mr H. Kirkwood and Mr W. McCulloch, on the outside, complete the known people in this typical group of the period.

Life in Helensburgh involves regular consideration of the climate, and as we approach the end of this book the weather must make a last appearance. Back in around 1910 the Fruin Water was frozen solid and people gathered to walk on it – not skating or curling, but in day shoes, long skirts and with walking sticks, quite often taking the dog for a walk.

The first sign of spring is usually the appearance of the cherry blossom on the roadside trees which have been a feature of the town throughout this century. They were first planted before 1914 as the policy of Dr Ewing Hunter, a town councillor, and a doctor at the Hermitage Auxilliary Hospital. Some streets are white, others pink – in 1961 this was the pink view down Colquhoun Street towards the West Kirk.

On Craigendoran Pier in the Summer of 1947, Mrs W.F. Robertson and Miss (Nanny) Reid lean on a barrow, awaiting boarding instructions for the next steamer to Greenock. Presumably not the PS *Jeannie Deans* whose steep gangway, caused by a high tide, can be seen, as there are other passengers at the end of the pier. Life in the period we have been looking at revolved around the comings and goings of the Clyde Steamers and railways, and all goods and baggage arrived and departed on the barrows along the piers and platforms.

Nine
Looking Ahead to 2002

And finally, as the Burgh of Helensburgh looks beyond the Millennium to its own bicentenary, and also to the centenary of The Hill House – both in 2002 – we conclude with a quick look at recent works which will contribute to the future and prosperity of the town. As Walter Blackie was patron of the young architect Charles Rennie Mackintosh, so now The Hill House provides an opportunity, in the atmospheric former guest room, for young designers to display their talents and sell their works. The 1999 season has showcased the works of Tim Krapp with his 'voyeur' chair and 'wanderer' table, Ben Huggins' pedestal, Phil Atrill's water drawing No.18 and blue glass, and landscape gold leaf vases by Belinda Hornsey.

This new building for Lomond School was designed by Ian McKellar, an architect who is a member of staff in his other guise of graphic communications teacher, with G.D. Lodge and Partners as executive architects. It has replaced older buildings and one that had suffered severe fire damage. At the head of John Street it combines the features of surrounding buildings and local construction details. It also makes the school a much more close-knit complex for the first time, as the new building is joined to the 1879 old hall.

Helensburgh Lawn Tennis Club has occupied a site between West Princes, King, and Suffolk Streets since 1884. An ambitious scheme in 1997 was funded jointly by the club and the Lottery Sports Fund with support from the Lawn Tennis Association, resulting in seven courts with all-weather playing surfaces and floodlighting. This clubhouse has all facilities and was designed by local architect Lawrence Hill of the Macdonald Williams Partnership.

Replacement of the Templeton Library was planned and begun under the former Dumbarton District Council in 1995 through a design and build contract with A. Trail and Sons Ltd and Alan Berry, architect for the structure of the library and adjacent Housing Association flats. It was fitted out and opened by Argyll and Bute Council in 1998 as Helensburgh Library. Much-enhanced access, display and technical facilities are adding to the cultural assets of the town.

A last look at the Hill House Design Exhibition, showing also the form of the room, the Mackintosh glass lights in the door and the stencilled walls. Exhibits are Peter Harvey's 'tongue in cheek' chair, El Ultimo Grito's 'mind the gap' table, Jan Miln's printed velvet stool and an aluminium coat stand by MDW.

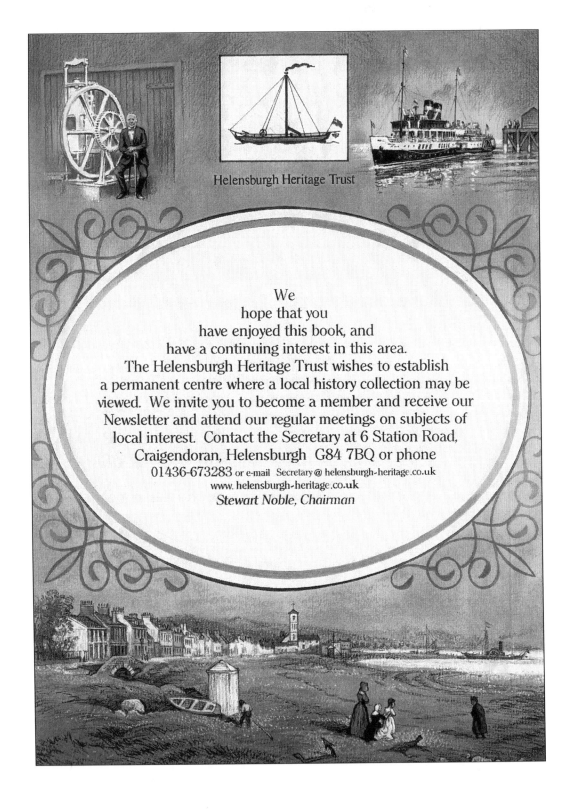

Helensburgh Heritage Trust

We
hope that you
have enjoyed this book, and
have a continuing interest in this area.
The Helensburgh Heritage Trust wishes to establish
a permanent centre where a local history collection may be
viewed. We invite you to become a member and receive our
Newsletter and attend our regular meetings on subjects of
local interest. Contact the Secretary at 6 Station Road,
Craigendoran, Helensburgh G84 7BQ or phone
01436-673283 or e-mail Secretary @ helensburgh-heritage.co.uk
www. helensburgh-heritage.co.uk
Stewart Noble, Chairman